Road Map

A Step-by-Step Process for Automating Marketing Success

G. Thomas Holland

DEDICATION

To all the business owners who
wanted to do their own thing their own way
and make a living doing so.

CONTENTS

Acknowledgments   i

Introduction   1

1   Know Where You Are   10

2   Set Your Goals   17

3   Set Your Sales Funnel   21

4   Draft the Plan   31

5   Create Your Offers   36

6   Automate Your Success   43

7   Develop Your Reporting Program   50

8   Develop an Editorial Calendar   58

9   Plan For Traffic   63

10   Take It to the Next Level   71

ACKNOWLEDGMENTS

For Courtney and the everyday support and motivation;
for Owen and the things you teach me;
for my family for always being there with love —
thank you.

INTRODUCTION

I wrote this book because 80% of all businesses fail within their first five years of operation, and because a rock star's affinity for M&M's shows us a way to prevent that.

Let me explain.

According to a 2016 survey published by Babson College, only 20% of all new businesses remain in operation after five years of existence. The survey found that this statistic was remarkably consistent over the course of several decades. In fact, several severe economic downturns did little to affect this seemingly concrete outcome. The survey also found that one of the top reasons 80% of new businesses fail stems directly from a failure to effectively market their product or service. In short, a majority of companies will go out of business because of a failure to properly market their business.

Business owners and entrepreneurs are a funny group. They'll work 80 hours a week running their own business so they don't have to endure a 40-hour, 9-to-5 workweek. They are visionaries, dreamers, and risk takers. They are the drivers of the global economy, and they are people I thoroughly enjoy working with and helping to achieve their dreams. I believe the world is better off with empowered entrepreneurs working to bring their visions to reality, and this book is for anyone looking to take the risk of starting or growing their business. I have made it my personal mission to help those who strive to achieve abundance through their passion.

Having worked with hundreds of small business owners, I have come to believe that the primary reason 80% of businesses fail within their first five years of existence is due to a lack of proper marketing and planning. This belief not only comes from my firsthand experience working with and advising all varieties of existing and new businesses, but also from the fact that businesses fail at a consistent rate no matter the economic environment. I wanted to write a book that would help the average business owner avoid common mistakes with marketing, and that would give them tools to overcome those issues.

The average small business owner has a good to great product or service. They see an opening in the market, and they are taking a step to take advantage of it. What they are most likely lacking, though, is a well-coordinated plan to market their product or service to their prospective clients. Businesses consistently fail because they don't bring in enough money from sales. Marketing's sole function is to start that sales process. If your sales are lacking, your marketing is probably lacking as well.

But how the hell do M&M's play any role?

They don't, directly. But to understand why I felt compelled to include them in this book, we need to learn a little bit about David Lee Roth.

During the 1980s, the rock band Van Halen was one of the top touring bands in America. The band would regularly play for crowds of more than 50,000 people, and the shows were just as big as the crowds and their fans' hairstyles. The spectacular events included pyrotechnics, lights, stage props, and multiple other trappings. These concerts were some of the biggest ever conceived and produced at the time, and they were incredibly technical and complex to execute.

Back then, the average headlining rock band would typically arrive at a venue with two to four semi-trailers packed with all the needed show equipment. As David Lee Roth recounted in the early 2000s, during their tours, the band usually required 18 to 22 semis to transport all the necessary technical, electrical and other gear. But the amount of material needed to execute a Van Halen show wasn't the only extraordinary thing. The Van Halen technical rider — the document outlining every single need of the band to produce one of their legendary concerts — was more than 1,000 pages long. It included detailed schematics, electrical specifications, and other protocols.

Adding to the overall complexity of the Van Halen tours was the fact that the band was bringing their show to smaller venues that were not experienced with productions of such caliber and complexity. Van Halen wasn't just going to Los Angeles, Chicago, and New York — they were performing in smaller towns such as Boulder, Colorado. These smaller-market venues had typically never seen such a high-level technical rider.

When the tour started, Van Halen's first shows experienced severe technical issues, and it quickly became clear that the venue personnel were not fully reading or complying with the band's technical rider, which would be sent to them in advance. Not only were the shows not living up to expectations, but the tour's own technical staff didn't have the capacity to review the entire venue's setup upon arrival before the show began.

What the band realized they needed was a quick way to determine whether everything in the technical rider had been fulfilled. Because there were so many electrical components, technical components, and other items involved, they couldn't personally review each item one by one. They needed a simple yet effective method to figure out whether their demands were in place immediately upon arrival at the concert location.

Enter brown M&M's.

It was lead singer David Lee Roth who had this idea for determining, upon arriving at a venue, whether a show's setup would be up to par. As Roth recounted in a later story, he had the idea after speaking with guitarist Eddie Van Halen. His idea was to bury a simple instruction about two-thirds of the way into the technical rider. The direction was that the venue was to stock the band's dressing room with a bowl of M&M's candies with all the brown M&M's removed. And while some people may chalk this requirement up to the demands of a spoiled rock star, the stipulation is actually a genius management method.

David Lee Roth had figured out a simple way to determine, with a single glance, whether the technical instructions had been followed. All he had to do to check the readiness of the production upon arriving at the next concert location was look for his bowl of M&M's. If no bowl of candy was present or if brown M&M's were included, he knew something was wrong and would immediately want to speak to the venue management team. He knew that he didn't have the time to check each and every part of the system, and in reality, it wasn't his job to do so. All he needed to know was whether one element was wrong, and that would be cause enough to stop everything and immediately demand a review.

I bring up this example because when you are a business owner, you're wearing many hats within the business. You're the chief executive officer, the chief marketing officer, head of customer service, and probably even the janitor. You don't have time to spend agonizing over multiple marketing reports filled with minutiae. You don't have time for much of anything more than an hour here or there.

The ideal solution, then, is to create a marketing plan that is easy to put into place and even easier to quickly review for sustainability and profitability. The faster you can determine which elements of your marketing plan are working and which aren't, the faster you can then address them and start improving your plan. Just like David Lee Roth and his bowl of M&M's, your key to success lies in an easy-to-use and easy-to-review reporting system.

The good news for business owners is that today's plethora of marketing communication tools makes it easier than ever to create the equivalent of the bowl missing the brown M&M's. Not only is it faster and simpler to identify and calculate the end results of your marketing efforts, but these tools offer automation features that will help you make more money without additional effort.

If you're reading this book, chances are high that your business is not making the kind of money you want to make or believe you should be making. Simply ask yourself right now: Could my marketing plan and/or department be producing better results? If your answer is in any way affirmative, this book is the right tool to help you address that discrepancy. This book offers an honest, straightforward and robust approach to developing a well-coordinated marketing plan that can help you achieve your goals and make more money.

The book is designed to be a step-by-step approach to developing, implementing, and scaling a sustainable marketing program. Here's what you can expect from each chapter:

Step 1: Know Where You Are will walk you through the process to understand how well your current marketing program is working. Before you set out on a road trip, build a building, or develop any strategy for success, you need to understand where you are currently — specifically, what you do really well and what your success looks like.

Step 2: Set Your Goals will show you how to figure out what goals you want to achieve and the method for ensuring those goals are attainable. As in any road trip, there is an end destination. Once you've set up your goals, the next step is to get your hands dirty and truly develop your business around your plan and your goals.

Step 3: Set Your Sales Funnel will help you solidify your sales funnel and become crystal clear on what it is you do at different service prices and service levels. It will also clear up how a customer will move from being aware of you but not making any purchases to becoming a die-hard customer who talks about you to other people.

Step 4: Draft Your Plan will show you how to start developing a plan and creating the basic structure of your core campaign. You'll see how goal setting influences your marketing plan, and what steps you need to take to start automating your success.

Step 5: Create Your Offers talks specifically about your offers. You'll develop a lead magnet and tripwire offer, and learn how these two elements are the key to building your sales and database of clients.

Step 6: Automate Your Success deals exclusively with automating "ascension" — using digital tools to automate the progression from a client first hearing about you all the way through becoming one of your best customers. This chapter is the most important, but can only be used after you have read through and completed the previous ones.

Step 7: Develop A Reporting Program shows you how to develop a reporting program that clearly identifies the areas that need attention from your marketing team. You will also learn how we look at the goals and success metrics from earlier chapters, and then develop a way to report how well you are progressing toward those goals.

Step 8: Develop an Editorial Calendar will teach you how to develop an editorial calendar for your digital marketing plan that will give you themes and context for speaking with your customers each month. Having an editorial calendar will help you determine the themes of your sales and the themes of the communications you will have with your clients. Too often, business owners and entrepreneurs don't fully develop an editorial calendar. You'll see it when they stop emailing their customers, the reason being that they simply don't know what to say. By having a plan, you'll have a monthly, weekly, or potentially even daily thing to talk to your customers about, allowing you to continue to serve them.

Step 9: Plan For Traffic shows you not only how to find new sources of customers, but how to craft messages proven to intrigue people into learning more about your service or product.

Step 10: Take It To The Next Level tells you about an opportunity to take your efforts to the next level.

At the end of the day, this book is designed to provide a step-by-step path for people looking to develop a marketing plan that will automate their success. My goal is that every person who reads this book comes away with an understanding of how to develop and implement a plan that all but ensures that their business will not become part of the 80% of businesses that fail within their first five years. It is a distillation of hundreds of client experiences and close to 20 years in the digital marketing space, and it is my effort to help everyone courageous enough to run or market their own company.

Now, let's get started.

STEP 1

KNOW WHERE YOU ARE

How much does it cost, on average, for you to get a new customer?

How much money will you make, on average, from that customer?

If you know the answers to these two questions, you should be happy to know that you are well on your way toward developing a successful marketing program. If you don't, you will soon learn why knowing these values will help you toward developing a marketing program that all but ensures your success.

When you start devising any marketing program, whether simple or complex, your first step is to develop an understanding of where your business is starting from. This baseline will not only serve as a measuring stick to gauge all of your future results, but it will also give you the opportunity to take an inventory of your business strengths, weaknesses, and performance when it comes to marketing and revenue. Any successful marketing or business development program will extensively measure the inputs and outputs that the system produces. If your business currently has no system in place to measure your results, you don't need to worry. We will discuss later how you can set those systems up.

The amount you pay to acquire a customer and how much they are worth to you on average are the most important numbers a business owner should know about their operation. They are the numbers that will dictate your marketing plan, your testing, and your budget allocation, among other actions. These values also make judging the performance of any marketing campaign incredibly easy. Like Van Halen's effort to simplify a complex system, we are creating our bowl of M&M's.

Let's take a closer look at these values, what they mean, and how you can use them.

The most important value for your business is your **Cost per Acquisition**, or CPA. This value represents what your business spends or what it costs, on average, to acquire a new paying customer. To calculate your business's CPA, you simply divide the total amount of money spent on the marketing campaign by the number of customers who purchased as a result of that campaign. While calculating this value across your entire business will provide a baseline CPA that you can use, it will be much more beneficial for your business to determine and continue to evaluate the CPA for your individual marketing channels and campaigns.

Determining the CPA for each channel and campaign will provide a better working knowledge of your operations than just having a general one for all of your customers and marketing efforts. For example, a highly successful campaign within a single channel could greatly skew the average results in such a way that your average CPA is not truly accurate or representative. This could have a detrimental effect on your decisions when it comes to adjusting your budgets following your reviews.

It's also important to differentiate CPA from **Cost per Lead** (CPL) value. CPL is a helpful measurement for understanding how much it costs to bring cold audiences — people who know nothing about you or your business — into your system. A lead is much different from a buyer or customer, though. Leads haven't taken that important step of having a financial transaction with your business, so while it's nice to know how much it costs to have a new lead in your system, it doesn't help you better understand what's generating your sales.

While CPA is an incredibly helpful metric, it works best with another value that helps determine what your average customer is worth to you over the course of their relationship with your business.

The other value you need to know is the **Average Lifetime Customer Value**, or ALCV. This number is calculated simply by dividing the total number of sales made by the total number of customers.

ALCV gives you an understanding of how much each customer is truly worth to you on average, but it's important to note that this value is dependent on the time interval you are measuring. ALCV shows you how much revenue you can reasonably expect from the client overall, **but not how soon you will see that income**. For example, some businesses have exceptionally long customer lifetimes. Medical professionals could expect to see a client for years or even decades. Conversely, other businesses might only see some customers once. This short customer lifetime would not necessarily alter the ALCV.

A great way to shed some additional light on the ALCV would be to calculate the **Average Customer Monthly Spend** (ACMS). This value is in our nice-to-know category — it's helpful to calculate, but your business's success doesn't hinge on knowing the value. By understanding how much you can expect to see in revenue per month from an average customer, you can better pace your marketing spends.

After you've calculated your CPA and ALCV, you can then start evaluating the starting efficiency of your existing marketing program. You simply check each campaign's (or channel's) ALCV and determine whether it is higher than the corresponding CPA. If a campaign's ALCV is higher than the CPA, you would continue that campaign or begin to scale it. On the other hand, if a campaign's ALCV is lower than the CPA, you would want to stop or immediately review the campaign in question. It's that simple, and you should now see why calculating CPA and ALCV values across your entire business doesn't present a truly accurate picture of how your marketing is working.

As a secondary report, you might want to consider

comparing each campaign's CPA with the ACMS. This report will show you how much monthly revenue you can reasonably expect from the money spent to acquire a new customer. Your business can sustain a campaign that has a CPA higher than its ACMS, but your end goal should be to have your customer's first purchase pay for the cost of acquisition. This report is also helpful for cash flow planning purposes and Return on Marketing Investment reporting.

We've talked a fair amount about useful stats up to this point, but there is additional insight into your business that can be very helpful in making your long-term plans. This information is not nearly as easy to develop, and in fact takes almost as much of a gut sense about your customers and business as it does actual values.

Most businesses have one of the following problems when it comes to their customer base: They either don't have enough, or they don't have enough high-impact clients. Many businesses, including ones that are younger or just starting out, will typically take on smaller projects or clients to increase their sales volume or capacity. They either never reach full capacity and make the mistake of marketing to these "beginner customers," or they reach their capacity and don't see an easy way to increase revenue. This is where you'll be well served by doing a deep dive into your customer base and finding your "Pareto" customers.

For those of you who never took Econ 101, the Pareto principle is a law that stems from a naturally occurring pattern in nature where 80% of the outcomes in a system come from only 20% of the inputs. The converse is also true, meaning that 80% of your inputs will account for only 20% of your business. Because this proportion occurs naturally in business systems, you can reasonably expect to plan for it and can design your marketing programs to account for such results. While understanding the ALCV for all of your clients on average is helpful, you can really take your marketing program to the next level by finding the ALCV and CPA of your 20% customers.

Take a moment to think about your customer base. Who are the 20% who account for 80% of your revenue? Start considering how they are different from your 80% clients, and how you might put that information to use within your marketing plan. You might find that your best clients all came from a single campaign or channel, for example, so scaling that campaign might yield exponential results for your business.

You can also review those 80% clients to find any commonalities they might have. What patterns can you find, and how can you extrapolate that information into working intelligence for your marketing campaigns? If you know that a majority of your small-scale customers came from a certain campaign or channel, you could then stop that program and focus instead on your higher-paying clients. You should also note that the Pareto principle doesn't just apply to revenue — you will also find it present when it comes to customer service needs. I'm sure you know of the 20% of your clients who demand 80% of your time as well. Is there a way you could find less intensive clients to work with from your targeted marketing campaign? Probably.

By understanding how well or poorly your marketing system is currently operating, you put yourself and your business in a better position for success in the long term. As a business owner, you have to know or have a solid approximation of your CPA and ALCV. It is from this knowledge that you can make truly sound decisions when it comes to refining your marketing campaigns. The legendary marketer Dan Kennedy has said that in the end, the business that will win is the business that can afford to spend the most to acquire a client. While later chapters will discuss strategies to increase your ALCV (thus allowing you the luxury of affording a higher CPA), right now you have the first basic tools to evaluate your marketing efforts. We have a starting point. Now, we need to know where we want to end up.

STEP 2

SET YOUR GOALS

Any great road trip has a starting point and an end point. In the previous chapter, we covered determining your starting point, evaluating how well or poorly your marketing plan is currently working, and some ways to measure that. In this chapter, we will cover goals, or the end destination you ultimately want to arrive at. Having goals is a necessity for any marketing plan, because you need to have some end point established to measure your efforts against. Setting ideal goals can be very helpful toward your actual achievement of them. Conversely, poor goal setting can have a detrimental effect on your business.

When I work with businesses in creating goals, I follow a simple yet effective goal-setting framework called the S.M.A.R.T. criteria to establish our end point. Each letter stands for a principle you want to ensure your goal abides by in order for it to be as well defined and as likely to succeed as possible.

Specific. Your goals should be specific. Not only should the end result be specific, but the target area of concern should be well identified as well.

A specific goal would be any monetary value. For example, a goal of "making more money" by itself is not a specific goal. A more specific goal would be "growing my business revenue by $250,000 from existing clientele." This growth goal gives you an exact idea of what the end point should be, and also specifies where that growth will come from.

Measurable. Your goal should quantify the progress you are looking to produce.

Numerical goals are great because they are easy to measure — either your outcome met the number or it didn't. But sometimes people set goals that are either immeasurable or not quantifiable, and that leads to problems.

For example, a goal of "having more people find our website" is not a measurable goal in the sense that it's way too broad and doesn't have a useful quantifiable element to it. You could undertake a lot of campaigns and efforts to try to reach that goal, but actually accomplishing it would be hard because it is a poorly defined goal. A better example would be a goal of "increasing organic traffic to our website by 30%." This sets the value you are looking to attain (30%), and it is a goal you can measure with an easy-to-use website analytics tool such as Google Analytics.

Assignable. Your goal should have at least one person who is responsible and accountable for its completion.

Accountability is an important feature of a great goal, as it clarifies who is responsible for the goal being met. That person should also understand clearly that they are the one responsible and should know exactly what is being asked of them. Assigning a goal doesn't accomplish anything if the person it is assigned to doesn't know or understand what you are tasking them with. If your business has more than one person who is responsible for your marketing efforts, it is acceptable to assign the goal to an entire department, but you still want to designate one person who is responsible for the overall achievement of the goal.

Realistic. Your goal should be within the reach of your organization given your available resources.

Realistic goals are the ones that can sometimes prove the hardest to set. As I mentioned before, business owners and entrepreneurs are dreamers and visionaries. These people already have high expectations, but their goals might not be grounded in reality. Setting realistic goals based on your resources is an absolute must.

For example, a startup might set a goal of "becoming a unicorn" (a startup venture worth more than $1 billion that is still privately held). While an admirable goal, it's probably not realistic, especially considering the product or service the business provides. The odds of having a unicorn lawn care or hair salon business are about as likely as winning the lottery. An established business would be much better served with a goal that is within reach but is still challenging enough that success is not simply assured.

Time-related. Your goal must have a specified date of achievement for measuring progress.

Typically, a good or great goal will be one that has a due date or expiration date. Having a time frame on your goal is helpful because it provides a setting from which you can plan and operate. Time frames for goals are best set at the quarterly and yearly marks, but can vary depending on your sales cycle and other factors.

When it comes to developing your goals for your business and marketing plan, you should also consider goals you have tried to achieve in the past and potentially revisit them. You might find that your old goals were sound in meaning but lacking in expression. Reframing a goal might be the missing piece needed to actually achieve it.

For example, I know of a lot of businesses that set goals and think they are goals worth measuring and achieving, but the goals are nothing more than an expression of an effort. These goals typically sound something like, "We will start social media soon." While this is a goal, it is essentially meaningless and measureless — all you are saying is that you will try something but not hold yourself to any results.

In summary, using the S.M.A.R.T. criteria to create your goals can be very helpful in not only identifying the actual goals you and your associates want to achieve, but also in increasing the likelihood of achieving them.

STEP 3

SET YOUR SALES FUNNEL

Up to this point, we have established both our baseline measurements for the key performance indicators of our marketing efforts as well as the end goals we are working to achieve. The next step is to create or solidify your sales funnel.

A sales funnel is the entire set of processes and marketing messages a business will use to advance a customer from not knowing anything about the business at all to purchasing the most expensive product or service it offers. Businesses have varying sales funnels in terms of levels, price points, and even the number of funnels themselves. What they all have in common, though, is that they provide the client with a next step to take or purchase to make after they've become a buying customer.

The key to success is to have a sales funnel that presents reasonable steps up from the last purchase. You don't want to overwhelm your clients with too much of an increase from one level to the next, as it will have a chilling effect on your sales flow.

This sales funnel framework is an incredibly important element to design *before* you start any marketing efforts, because it also helps you structure and solidify the marketing automation elements that are so critical for automating success. When you establish in advance the progression each client should make, you then put yourself in a position where you can automate that sales ascension. Making sales automatically is an incredibly powerful capability to have in your business.

When you create your sales funnel, it's important to understand two things. First, in business, the simple way to make more money is to **have more customers buying more stuff more often**. It's truly that simple. A well developed sales funnel will help you automate customers buying more stuff, more often — pieces of the more revenue equation.

It's also important to understand the different kinds of customers and which customers your sales funnel will affect the most. Any business will have three kinds of customers: cold, warm, and hot. Your sales funnel's strength in automating the sales between your warm and hot clients is the key to making more money and enjoying more success. Because you might not be familiar with this idea, let me define the three types of customers.

A cold customer is someone who has never heard about you and doesn't know you exist. These are the kinds of clients you will present with **lead magnets** in your marketing effort. A lead magnet is something of value that you give to the potential client free in an effort to (1) educate them about your business and services, and (2) get them to stop shopping and start considering purchasing with your business. We will cover lead magnets in-depth later on, as these are important elements that need special consideration by themselves.

A warm customer is someone who knows of you and may have even opted in to your lead magnet, but — and this is crucial — has not yet purchased anything from you. A warm client may be ready to buy, but money hasn't exchanged hands yet. Your marketing campaigns will regularly present tripwire offers, or offers to warm customers that judge their readiness to buy. After a purchase has been made, your sales funnel and the corresponding automated elements will start the process of indoctrinating the customer and preparing them for the next purchase automatically.

And finally, a hot customer is someone who has financially purchased something from you. This behavior is key — money has to have exchanged hands before a customer can reach hot status. And once a customer has reached hot status, you then try to progress more and more with them sales-wise until they stop buying.

You should also know that of the three kinds of customers, hot customers (or hot traffic) are the only customers that you can show sales offers to without the standard and introductory tripwire offers. Because they have purchased from you before, their barrier to doing so is much lower than it is for your warm or cold customers.

Understanding the different customer types is helpful for understanding how these customers will experience your sales funnel via your marketing campaigns.

One of my mentors best described a sales funnel as the stages of dating. A good sales funnel should progress upon each previous interaction slightly, similar to when you're beginning to date someone. You would never ask your date for their hand in marriage on the first date if you truly wanted to have the best possible relationship with that person. The sequence is all off. Instead, you take things step by step, moving forward when both parties are ready.

It's easier to showcase a funnel than it is to speak about one in theoretical terms, so let's consider an example for a lawn care services company. This type of business might have a sales or service funnel as follows.

- A free consultation and service plan (**lead magnet**)

- A $27 quick-cut service that features a single lawn mowing (**tripwire**)

- A $47 one-time service featuring an application of fertilizer in spring and fall (**profit maximizer**)

- A $97 mowing and treatment service that adds upon the previous mowing service by including several upsell services to address additional issues with the lawn (**upsell**)

- A high-end, $127 monthly service that includes

lawn mowing, treatment services, and irrigation maintenance throughout the year (**big ticket**)

In this sales funnel, a cold customer, or cold traffic, is offered a free consultation and service plan via the marketing campaign. This lead magnet (consultation) is something of value that aims to get the client to stop researching and start buying (the $27 quick-cut service tripwire). The lead magnet also allows you to collect that client's information for ongoing marketing efforts and to help you build your database.

After the client has moved from a cold customer to a warm one, we will gauge their readiness to buy as soon as we can with a tripwire offer. In this case, the tripwire is a reasonably priced entry service that features the company's basic offering. The tripwire should allow people to "test drive" their experience with you and get a sense of your product or service and what it's like working with you. A great tripwire offer will have a satisfaction guarantee that takes all the potential harm out of purchasing. Ideally, your tripwire is something that is not only logical to buy, but something that is as easy as possible to buy. You want to have as simple a process as possible for your tripwire offers.

Before we move on here in the discussion of a sales funnel, it's important to note that the deeper you get into your sales funnel, the less likely the services, products, or packages will change. That means that your lead magnets and tripwire offers will not be set forever, but rather that you should expect to test many variations of them when optimizing your funnel or marketing program.

The moment a customer purchases, you'll then want to include an immediate profit maximizer offer. These are additional offers that reinforce the tripwire but also increase the amount of money you are netting during the transaction. Remember, to make more money, your customers have to buy more stuff, and a profit maximizer offer is a great way to do that after your customer has started buying. The profit maximizer should be an easy add-on to the tripwire and make logical sense for inclusion.

After the client has purchased the tripwire and potentially the profit maximizer, you will want to start presenting upsell offers. Such offers will push the customer deeper into your sales funnel by presenting higher-value offers and giving them the opportunity to take advantage of those new offers. You can vary when you start trying to upsell the client, but my recommendation is to do so only after they have used your product and indicated they are happy with it. A customer shouldn't be upsold before they have used a tripwire offer, nor should they be shown any upsell offers before you get feedback from them. Your service process needs to include customer feedback elements that will help influence your marketing. In this case, after someone has experienced the tripwire offer, they should be given a link to a survey that will give them the opportunity to tell you what they thought. If their answers are positive, you would then want to try to upsell as soon as possible.

After the tripwire purchase is over, you will want to start gauging how receptive your lead is toward moving to the next step. Customer relationship management (CRM) software is great for this, and tools such as Infusionsoft can help you automate the process of following up on the first experience and beginning the prospect of the next purchase. Each sales funnel progression would follow this process. Once a successful purchase has been made, the CRM or sales team would follow up to make sure everything went well, and would start the education toward the next purchase option and gauge the customer's likelihood of pursuing that option.

Finally, the last step of a sales funnel would be a big-ticket product or service. This is the highest-value and highest-priced service that you offer, and it's the end goal for all of your customers after they enter your sales funnel. Your big-ticket item could even be a continuity offer (services provided monthly) that would ensure consistent income versus higher amounts of money coming in less frequently. Your hot clients should be the only ones who get marketed these offers, as they are the most likely to purchase a higher-end product or service from you.

With this example, you can see that there is a progression from each service to the next that offers more services at a higher price. This allows the customer to find the right blend of services for an acceptable cost. By offering multiple options, you are increasing the likelihood the customer will end up purchasing from or working with you.

As noted before, sales funnels can vary widely with regard to prices, levels of progression, and even the number of funnels themselves. Your sales funnel might simply exist for a segment of your customers. For example, restaurants would usually only have a regular menu, but a catering operation within the business would benefit from having a sales funnel that offers different levels of services. Other businesses that offer a variety of services might have funnels for each service that would then automatically "push" a hot client from one funnel into a lead magnet campaign for another to try to extend their purchasing.

At this point, you are likely realizing how important an established sales funnel can be in helping your business grow. You might also be realizing that being able to test variations of your sales funnel is a determining factor in how quickly you become successful (or don't). As most successful marketers know, your sales funnel is the key to making real money.

Another advantage of a sales funnel is that it allows you to standardize your services, and this then allows you to standardize your operations. After you have a set of common standards for each product or service you provide, you can then generate more revenue, as you have cut down on the amount of time needed to service a client. Offering custom solutions is fine, but that kind of personalized service needs to be at the top of your price range and sales funnel.

At this point, you should start developing or solidifying your funnel, understanding that there are not set ways to develop a funnel. My advice would be to start by trying to draw out on paper or a whiteboard what you think your funnel looks like or what you would want it to be. The easiest way is to draw a cone with the large part at the top and the small part at the bottom, and then draw horizontal lines within the cone for each level or progression your sales funnel has. Lay out your products or services at each level, and indicate the prices for each. Consider enlisting the assistance of your team (should you have one) to ensure you are not missing anything.

If you don't know whether you have a sales funnel or if you want to start fresh, I would suggest another way to develop an outline of your sales funnel. One exercise is to consider what you would create if you had to have a sales funnel that offered products at price points of $1, $10, $100, $1,000, and even $10,000 and beyond. This forces you to think about packages you could offer at different price points and how you would deliver them. As shown in our previous example, a lawn can be mowed at many different prices.

What you want to make sure you have in your funnel at this point are your big-ticket offers, your upsell offers, and your tripwire and profit maximizer offers. Right now, you just need to focus on (1) the offers that people will end up buying, and (2) the offers that customers will see to push them into the next purchase toward the big-ticket offer. Such customer experiences are incredibly important to have mapped out, because once you have determined what offers your customers should see after they have purchased something, you will have created the outline for the ascension automation plan. The plan will allow you to program your marketing tools to start making sales offers automatically and start making money automatically.

Developing a sales funnel and variations for testing is

a process that can be as in-depth as you would like. In fact, entire books have been written about this subject alone, but our purpose here is simply to ensure you have a general idea of what a sales funnel is and what yours looks like so you can start a marketing campaign. Testing can come later, and you will find that the more time you spend on this part of your business, the more rewards you are likely to see. At the very least, you need to have tripwire offers established along with profit maximizers, and know which offers you would then want to show each corresponding buyer in an effort to get them to purchase your big-ticket offer.

After you have solidified your sales funnel, you are ready to start putting into place the automation pieces that will turn your business into a money machine operating on a proven road map.

STEP 4

DRAFT THE PLAN

By this point, we have established our baseline numbers, determined our end goal, and solidified our sales funnel. Our next step is to draft out the marketing plan — essentially, how we will get to our end goal from our starting point. The fastest way to get an idea of what you will have to accomplish with your marketing plan is to figure out how many high-ticket packages you would have to sell to meet your goal. If your goal is $1 million in new revenue this year and your highest-priced package is $5,000, then you know you need to acquire at least 200 new customers.

Once you know how many customers are needed for your goal, turn your attention to developing a **customer avatar**, or a written description of your average customer. This avatar can include many different elements, but at a basic level, it needs to highlight eight to 10 defining characteristics of your customers that (1) they all typically have in common, and that (2) make them different from the general population. Taking the time to develop these traits will be very helpful, as the more they are defined and accurately represent your client, the more resonance your marketing message will have with your target audience. It is also possible to segment your target audiences by these traits in most online advertising platforms, so this exercise will help you prepare for the development of your online advertising efforts as well.

Not all businesses are created equally, and it's highly likely your business doesn't have just one average customer. The reality is that you have many different customers, but your focus should be on developing three to five avatars for the 20% of your clients who make up 80% of your business. Three to five avatars should get you enough definition for marketing purposes while still accurately representing the target audiences you want to share your marketing message with.

The two most important elements an avatar should include are the customer's interests as well as their media consumption habits. Your avatars should define which media your customers consume the most or which online media they frequent. The idea here is to develop a list of channels your customers are most likely to use and thus where they're most likely to see your marketing message when you advertise. A simple survey to your customer base can help you start gleaning this information, or you could hold a focus group with some of your key customers to get ideas as well.

When forming your plan to reach the number of customers needed to hit your goal, your avatars will help you determine how many of each customer you can realistically expect to acquire. For example, you might find that you have four types of Pareto (20%) customers. If you know that you need 100 of these customers to reach your goal, you might realize that expecting an equal division of those 100 customers across the four customer types is not realistic. Based on your experience, you might know that you have much more opportunity to entice one of those four avatar types, so you should spend a majority of your efforts on them, as doing so will bring about a greater chance of success.

Once you understand how many of each client you must acquire for your goal, you have completed a major milestone in drafting your plan. Any marketing campaign has three pieces: the goal, the strategies, and the tactics. We've already established the end goal. By determining the number of clients you need to acquire or have purchase your big-ticket item in order to reach your end goal, you have developed your marketing campaign strategy. This strategy can change during your campaigns as needed if you are not pacing toward your goals, but having something to start with is more important than having nothing at all.

The last piece of the marketing plan you will need to develop are your tactics. For the purposes of this book, we will define tactics as the marketing channels used to present your lead magnet offers to cold traffic. The process of creating the offers you will present to cold traffic will be discussed more thoroughly in a later chapter, but for now, we will discuss how to select the media you will use for marketing your offers.

The biggest piece of advice I can give you in this realm is to consider how well your current sales funnel is working. If your funnel is very consistent at producing customers and you average higher than a 5-to-1 return on your marketing investment, then I would suggest you could look further than Facebook and Google AdWords for your media (provided you are already using those channels). If your sales funnel is newly developed and you don't have a proven track record of results, I would suggest you focus on Facebook and Google AdWords to start your cold traffic campaigns.

You will eventually add more traffic sources to your marketing mix, but you want to develop and test your sales funnel performance first, and these two platforms provide the fastest and cheapest means available of obtaining traffic. Once your marketing campaign and sales funnel are producing customers at the right numbers, you will add in more of the marketing channels identified in your customer avatars. You will then start testing the budget allotments for each platform to find the optimal mix for producing leads and clients.

At this point, you have determined how many clients you will need to reach your goal, what those clients look like, and through which channels you will communicate your cold traffic offers to those clients. You are getting closer to finishing the actual build-out of the campaign, even if it doesn't seem like it. The next step of developing your initial offers will be the last creative one you have to do, as the rest of the work (until you start reviewing your incoming data) is more administrative in nature.

STEP 5

CREATE YOUR OFFERS

After you have either created or solidified your sales funnel, you have ensured that once people become a buyer, you have a plan for additional offers and sales. While these parts are important to your business's overall effort to achieve automated success, they will never get used if your cold traffic never become customers. It's thus imperative that people become buyers in the first place, and that is why your lead magnet and tripwire offers are so crucial to your business. If these offers aren't enticing to your cold traffic, you will never have any long-term buyers.

As you start to consider what lead magnets and tripwires you will develop for your marketing campaigns, it's important to truly understand what each offer should accomplish and what each needs to include. Your offers will perform at a higher rate if you understand what they need to accomplish beyond just getting the contact information of a client or an entry sale.

The purpose of a lead magnet is to grab the attention of your cold traffic by speaking to their needs and giving them a reason to pay attention to you. People are interrupted with literally thousands of marketing messages throughout the day, and your message needs to be compelling enough to make them stop what they are doing (given that they were not expecting your message) and pay attention to you. An enticing lead magnet grabs people and gets them to consider how you might be able to help them. Results-based lead magnets do very well with cold traffic, as they show people how your product or service can bring about the results you lead with.

Your lead magnet offers also set the tone or voice that your clients experience from you. If you are a service professional who is branding yourself as a world-class expert, your lead magnet should incorporate that tone and feeling. The lead magnet is the perfect opportunity to showcase your expertise and start the indoctrination process of convincing a person to consider you as the solution to their problem.

Lead magnets can take many different forms and be various types of media. Your business can take any existing knowledge and package it into an easy-to-access format. This can range from a PDF e-book that your cold traffic can consume at their leisure to a video they can watch immediately.

There are three things to consider when creating your

lead magnet for use with your marketing campaign. First, what does your prospective client want? This can be something the client is either aware of or isn't, but the key to your success will be to identify a deficiency they are currently facing. The lead magnet needs to not only clearly identify what that deficiency is, but also what "pain" can result because of it. People respond much better to the prospect of missing out on something than they do to the prospect of getting something they already have. By identifying the pain, you can craft your message to resonate strongly with cold traffic.

The second thing is the solution to the pain point. Every problem needs an answer, and your lead magnet should start teasing what that solution might look like. You don't want your lead magnet to give away the solution to the problem; rather, it should suggest that your approach to the problem is the best one for the cold traffic to consider.

The last thing you need to consider when developing your lead magnet is how you can best show potential clients the value of working with you. Your clients will have a preferred method of communicating and taking in information, and you need to be mindful of that when creating your lead magnet.

Videos are a great way to tell any story and are highly effective in capturing people's attention. Videos are usually more expensive to produce than e-books or other types of media, and videos have a very short window of time to completely grab a customer's attention. Those two caveats noted, however, you should consider a decent video production effort to deliver your lead magnet. On the other hand, digital text files are usually faster and cheaper to produce. These files can often be derived from existing marketing content and can be implemented into a lead magnet asset at a swifter pace.

The most important thing to keep in mind when creating your lead magnet is that you need to get a person's contact info in exchange for their taking the lead magnet. You want to build your database with viable contacts, so your lead magnet needs to be good enough to justify a person handing over their contact information to you. People value their contact information — they won't just hand it out to anyone.

When it comes to the tripwire, the goal is to create an offer that is easy to buy, is something that limits the amount of risk, and that essentially gets your client to stop shopping by testing their readiness to buy. Making the tripwire easy to buy can be accomplished in a variety of ways. Whether digital transactions or purely analog ones, you will want to make sure you can measure how many of these offers you sell and from what marketing source they originated. If you are using multiple lead magnets, you will also want to make sure you can track which lead magnet your tripwire buyers originally came from. It's important to attribute the true source of the conversion to the lead magnet closest to the tripwire purchase versus the initial lead magnet, as this will provide a better understanding of your client's journey to becoming a paying client.

The most important element of the tripwire offer is the level to which it limits the amount of risk a buyer will undertake. The level of risk itself is based on both the price of the offer and any satisfaction guarantee that can help mitigate customer concerns or other issues. The price itself needs to be as entry-level as possible. There are different theories on pricing, but a decent rule of thumb is that your tripwire offer should be between $7 and $47. This is a low enough price that the buyer shouldn't experience sticker shock. If they do, then you haven't communicated your value in alleviating their "pain."

The second aspect of risk is the satisfaction guarantee element. What people are more interested in with any offer or purchase is what recourse they might have if the offer doesn't meet their expectation. The best approach to a tripwire offer is to make it as risk-free as possible. This usually means offering a 100% refund to anyone who is not fully satisfied. When you do offer a satisfaction guarantee, you want to make sure your marketing message makes this sales point as clear as possible, as you will have sales that you close because of this point alone.

The last piece of the tripwire puzzle is to test the client's readiness to buy. When presenting your warm traffic (as they have opted in to your marketing efforts, they are now no longer cold traffic) with your tripwire offer, you want to make crystal clear what the offer is and what they can expect if they purchase.

Now that you know what each entry offer needs to have, you can start developing those lead magnets and tripwires simultaneously — you don't want to develop these two independently. The reason you need to have both offers working together is that your tripwire offer will convert at a much higher rate when it is shown to a warm audience than it will when shown to a cold audience. By showing your lead magnet offer first, you are educating a customer about you and indoctrinating them, increasing the likelihood that they will purchase from you.

When devising your offers, it's important to create lead magnets and tripwires for the audiences you are targeting in your overall campaign. Just as no product or service is truly one-size-fits-all, to reach your goals, you need to have special offers for the different groups of people you are targeting.

For some service providers, it's hard to offer a tripwire given the cost of their service. Let's say you are a real estate attorney and your basic service package costs $1,500. You could have a great lead magnet but still find it difficult to sell your basic package because of the price point of your first service. What you would want to do is get creative and see whether there is some sort of product or service you could offer at a $50 to $100 price range that would let people "try you out" and get them to stop shopping around. This product could be anything from a group class to a recorded webinar — it just needs to be something that gives a person the opportunity to advance the relationship at their pace.

As a service provider, you could do a free consultation that lasts 30 to 60 minutes as a tripwire offer. What you're recognizing here is that people won't spend money with you, but will spend their time. Time is something of value and something that people can spend to indicate some level of interest. For example, if you're a tax attorney or an accountant, you could offer a 60-minute session wherein the end result is four action items to help your client move forward in developing better tax or accounting strategies. Even though there's no financial transaction involved, this person will have up-leveled their relationship with you by attending the session, and you will be giving them something in return. Producing the results of the session on a handout with an offer to get started on the next service package could be how you start the next step of selling to that person.

Some businesses, such as food service operations, don't have an extended sales funnel. They have just a menu, and it wouldn't be practical to try to get people to buy more items during each visit. In cases like these, it may be appropriate to combine your lead magnet and tripwire offer into the same thing, such as a coupon. Coupons are usually given away free (like a lead magnet), but they can also test the client's readiness to buy (like a tripwire). So, depending on the kind of business you own, your initial lead magnet and tripwire offers can vary greatly in form and value.

Now that you have created your initial tripwire and lead magnet offers, it is time to finish out your sales funnel by automating it. You have created all the steps in your sales funnel, and now you need to build out the pieces of the marketing machine that will automatically push your clients through those steps toward the next product or service they will be interested in.

STEP 6

AUTOMATE YOUR SUCCESS

After you have solidified your sales funnel and understand clearly the different levels of products or services you offer, your next step is to implement the automation of your ascension. "Ascension" is simply the word we use to describe the moment a customer reaches a higher level in your sales funnel by opting in or purchasing something beyond the initial lead magnet or tripwire offer.

The great thing about digital marketing is that once someone opts in to your system, you can market and sell to that person automatically with your company's customer relationship management (CRM) software. All the hard work you completed earlier has laid out "paths" that your customers will take after they have bought your tripwire offer. These paths should lead your warm traffic toward the eventual goal of buying your highest-ticket offer. So, the real power of your CRM comes from its ability to increase your sales by having people ascend deeper into your funnel without consistent and intensive labor on your part.

To better illustrate what this would look like, let's say you have a warm traffic customer who purchases your e-book that details your approach to a problem and your solution. When they purchase the book, a good ascension effort would not only deliver the product, but would also start delivering marketing materials to (1) reinforce the quality of their purchase, and (2) start suggesting additional (and higher-dollar) services that you offer. This ascension strategy could also then deliver other messages based on the actions your clients take — such as clicking on a link but not buying a product or service — to help continue the effort to sell them the next service.

Let's take a second to truly appreciate how powerful creating a system like this can be. The alternative is calling up each person who buys your book and saying, "Hey there, I want to thank you for buying the book. Here's an online course I think you'd find valuable. Would you be interested in buying? What questions do you have?" You don't want to do that individually — you would never get much done. You want to do that automatically.

Before you can develop and implement any ascension effort in your marketing campaign, you need to integrate a CRM that allows you to send out automated marketing messages to people in your database. You need three things available in such a tool. These three elements are critical to automating your success, and you shouldn't consider using a certain CRM if it doesn't have all three.

Need #1: It needs to be able to send out emails automatically based on a contact's actions in your system.

This might seem like a no-brainer, but there are in fact plenty of database tools out there that don't even allow you to send out emails to your contacts. You need to be able to program campaign emails (for the automation pieces) and send broadcast pieces (for ad hoc campaigns) to people within your database.

Need #2: It needs to enable you to automatically identify the people who are at each step in your sales funnel.

Another critical function of a CRM is the ability to mark up data so that when an action happens within your system, your built-in reporting can easily tell you not only where any individual person is in your sales funnel, but how many people are at each step.

One tool I have used consistently with clients is Infusionsoft, and it is a great platform for a number of reasons. One reason is that it has the ability to create and count "tags" that you can apply to contacts in your database.

With Infusionsoft, you could create a tag that you would apply to a contact when they ascend to the next step in your sales funnel. The tag would be added at the moment of purchase, and the previous step's tag would be removed. You could also create tags to indicate what communications a customer has received from ad hoc campaigns, or how they have responded to those campaigns. The possibilities, while not endless, do allow for some helpful approaches to managing and viewing your contacts and their progression through your sales funnel.

Need #3: Your CRM must have the ability to fulfill your orders *or* start the fulfillment process.

Because you are creating an integrated system, you will find it beneficial if your marketing machine and your sales-and-fulfillment machine are in the same place, or if they can at least talk to each other. This will make your job much less manual and your database much easier to maintain.

These three items are the must-haves when it comes to selecting a CRM. If your current CRM doesn't have these three tools, I would highly suggest switching to a different one. I would recommend Infusionsoft (note: I have been an affiliate sales partner of Infusionsoft in the past), but there are plenty of others out there, such as Maropost and MailChimp, that you should consider as well.

After you've selected your CRM, you then need to build out your automation sequences. So, let's work with a supposed client path to show what you would need to include at each step. For this example, our case study will be a food services attorney who wants to sell high-end consulting and retainer services. His sales funnel looks like this: a free e-book lead magnet, a $47 strategy session tripwire offer, a $997 self-guided legal course, and $3,997 monthly retainer services.

When someone opts in to get the e-book, the person

gets created as a contact in his system, is tagged as someone who has requested the lead magnet, and is then sent an email with the actual e-book or a link to download it. This is where the ascension automation begins.

Following the email that delivers the e-book, three follow-up emails should be sent in 24-hour intervals to the recipient, each with additional information to help them get the most out of the e-book. For example, you could send an email with additional insight, reading directions, or even supplemental videos for later chapters to help encourage reading or to further indoctrinate the reader. Note that in this example, the suggestion is three emails — you will have to do some testing to see what your audience responds best to, but you want to have a follow-up email strategy in place to help people with what you have already given them *before* you start selling them into the next product.

Once the indoctrination email campaign ends, you could then send a survey email to the lead to gauge how well they liked the book. Depending on how they respond to the survey, you would send them into a new email sequence. If they didn't like the book, you'd tag them as such in your CRM and could send them an email sequence with additional articles to further determine whether you can help them. At the end of this sequence, you would want to include a call to action to the $47 tripwire. Remember, just because someone didn't buy right away doesn't mean they won't buy later. If they don't buy at this point, you'd continue marketing to them with ad hoc campaigns and offers.

If the person did like the book, you would tag them as such and then move them into the $47 tripwire offer sequence.

After you have email sequences created and set up for each possible outcome of the $47 tripwire offer, you'd then move on to the next levels of the sales funnel (the $997 course and $3,997 retainer) and put in elements much like the ones we did before: tags in the CRM to describe what actions the client took, email sequences to push them into purchasing the next product or to deliver more value to their existing purchase, and then a call to action at the end of each appropriate sequence.

A simple rule of thumb would be to have up to seven automated emails programmed to be sent to anyone who purchases an offer, with the emails suggesting the next offer to them. You would need to tailor the delivery of these emails to fit within your sales cycle — obviously, you don't want to start sending out ascension emails before the client has even begun using your previous product or service.

At this point, there are two things to keep in mind. The first is that your ascension campaigns are going to be the biggest focus once you finally turn your machine "on," because this is where the majority of your actual money will be made. When you are first creating these ascension elements, you need to keep in mind that perfection is not needed at this early stage. Develop "functional" sequences and elements that are good enough for use with cold traffic, with the understanding that your client traffic through these sequences will show you what works and what doesn't.

Something that will help with your later reporting is the creation of reporting dashboards for each of the data markups you have for each stage. With my Infusionsoft clients, we simply generate saved contact searches for each tag that show which people are at each ascension level. We then add these stats to a reporting dashboard within the client's CRM, so that whenever they log in to their system, they know how many people are in their pipeline at any given moment.

After you have completed creating and implementing the ascension elements for each step of your sales funnel, you should really give yourself some credit for the work you've done. You've created an automatic sales machine and are one (big) step closer to automating your success!

STEP 7

DEVELOP A REPORTING PROGRAM

The most important ability you need to have as a business owner is the ability to quickly discern whether your marketing program is working (remember David Lee Roth?). Frankly, too many business owners just throw money away by trying marketing strategies that don't work. They may not understand what is happening with their marketing or what makes their marketing ineffective. That's why having an effective and simple reporting program is so vital.

Knowing what your CPA and ALCV stats are will help quickly and immensely in seeing whether your business is on sound footing. In a nutshell, if you spend less to get a buyer (CPA) than what that buyer is worth to you overall (ALCV), then you are moving in the right direction. However, if your clients are initially spending less than it costs to acquire them, it's possible your business may not be operating in a sustainable fashion (again, that's why it's critical to also understand your ALCV). The main characteristic you are looking for in a reporting program is simplicity.

One of the most valuable tools you can use with your business is Google Analytics. It is a free tool that Google offers to any website owner, and it allows you a wide variety of statistic reporting capabilities with regard to the visitors and actions on your website. There are similar programs available that offer variations (Matomo.org is a personal favorite), but the single feature your analytics reporting tool needs to offer is goal or conversion tracking. This feature allows you to set an end destination (a URL) within your website that you have defined as the desired goal. You can then track the number of website users who arrive at this end URL.

Earlier, I had you create lead magnet and tripwire offers. To start the development of your reporting program, you first need to consider how people will actually go about getting these offers, and how you can measure how many times that happens. For example, if you have a PDF lead magnet, you need to have a way to measure how many times that file gets downloaded. If your lead magnet involves the person calling in to redeem the offer (whether a lead magnet or tripwire), you need a way to record how many times the phone rings for that offer. By keeping the redemption methods simple, you make keeping track of the number of clients who have opted in to your marketing easier for yourself as well.

My recommendation for lead magnets is to have the actual magnet itself available "behind" or following the completion of an opt-in form. When you use an opt-in form to capture people's contact information, you will have the option of sending them to a web page after they've successfully completed the form. This page is commonly referred to as a "thank you" page, and **it should only be accessible by people who have completed the form**. The "thank you" page should have the link to the lead magnet file itself. All of your lead magnets need to have a thank-you page that people will be directed to upon completion of the opt-in form. You will also want to make sure that each lead magnet has its own thank-you page versus having a single thank-you page that all lead magnet traffic ends up visiting.

By now, you might be realizing that your thank-you pages will be the goal URLs you will set for your Google Analytics goal tracking. By setting your thank-you pages as the end destination URLs for your goal or conversion tracking, you will not only be able to see how many people are opting in to your lead magnet, but you will be able to break that number down by source and other characteristics. This allows you to see any number of stats, but our main purpose here is to see (1) how many people opted in to your lead magnet, and (2) from which source or link they did so.

After you or your team has configured the tracking for your lead magnets, you will want to set up your tracking for your buyers or first-time customers. You can use much of the same setup that we discussed before for your lead magnets — thank-you pages can be set up to start fulfillment for the customer while your website analytics tool will use these pages to keep track of the number of customers. Keep in mind that while most website analytics software systems are fairly robust, there will always be discrepancies, so having a second system to back up or audit your results would be ideal.

Also, if your business uses an all-in-one website solution or an online shopping cart tool for accepting payments, you probably have some sales reporting tools to begin with. If that is the case, you will want to consider what shopping cart and CRM system integrations are available and how you might be able to use the two together. You might not need to use a tracking tool like Google Analytics for keeping track of leads or opt-ins, but you will need to make sure that your shopping cart can keep track of sourcing your buyers into the system. You should still use some sort of tool to measure website visitor behavior, and Google Analytics is ideal for that.

Google Analytics allows you to set up automated reporting that will send you scheduled emails with reports attached as PDFs. I typically recommend setting your lead magnet opt-in reports to a weekly setting, delivered on a Monday morning for your review as the week starts. This reporting arrangement is something that the average computer user should be able to set up on their own, but some might find they need to hire outside help to make this piece of reporting automated.

Google Analytics is great for tracking goals and conversions from your website traffic. Although we live in an increasingly digital world, however, we have to account for "real world" (analog) events where people opt in to our systems outside of the normal digital channels. While people can use their phones to accomplish many things online, they can also place an old-fashioned phone call to learn more and opt in. What do you do for people like this?

Call-tracking technology sites such as CallRail.com are a great way to track the number of people who call in to opt in to your business from marketing. These tools are helpful in that they can record the calls (so you can tell whether it was a legitimate lead generation event), and in that they allow you to isolate and control for lead generation from digital campaigns.

CallRail, for example, uses something called "dynamic number insertion," which shows your web traffic a different phone number to call if they come from a predetermined source. This means you can have your regular phone number shown to organic traffic, or the people who just find you online naturally, and a different phone number shown to the purchased traffic who come from a campaign. This gives you greater certainty that a person came to you from an online campaign, and you can then mark up the client's record accordingly in your CRM. Some of these call-tracking tools even have integrations that you can use to account for these positive lead generation events in your Google Analytics account or your CRM's tagging system.

Using a call-tracking tool like this would even allow you to track results beyond just the campaign level. Some tools give users the ability to use multiple numbers for tracking, and this allows for results tracking at a more granular level. For example, if you were using Google

AdWords, you could review results by ad set or even keyword.

Call tracking is very powerful and a must-have for businesses that will see a lot of call-in traffic. It's also helpful for businesses that don't have a natural client survey period during the initial visit. You would expect, for example, to be asked at least one question about where you heard about the service provider when you first visit a dentist, a lawyer, or certain other businesses. You wouldn't expect to be asked this at a restaurant, though, and that's one example of where a call-tracking tool can be valuable.

At this point, you should now be able to track all of your lead magnet opt-ins and tripwire buyers, ideally by each marketing channel. The final piece of developing your CPA reports is to create a spreadsheet in Microsoft Excel or Google Sheets in which you pair up the amount of money you spent on each marketing channel with the number of opt-ins from each. This will allow you to automatically calculate your CPA. (Of course, this assumes you are keeping track of your marketing spends as you progress through your campaigns.)

To ensure proper reporting from Facebook, you or your team will need to install tracking software from Facebook's advertising tool called Facebook Pixels into your website. You want this tracking tool to be set up to register anyone who opts in to your lead magnet. You can try to do this yourself, but I've found it's often better to have a web team complete this task. Once installed, you can then set your reporting to be saved within the Facebook advertising manager for later review. You can also schedule these reports to be emailed to you on a regular basis. These basic reports will need to present your ad campaign's Cost per Acquisition.

At some point, after enough success, you will likely start using other traffic tools to market your business, and as you grow, your reporting will need to do so as well. Facebook's reporting tools mentioned earlier only work with Facebook traffic, so you will need to create reporting tools for your other sources.

Finally, you need to create your Average Lifetime Customer Value report. This is a report you won't have to prepare as frequently (maybe quarterly), but it will be helpful when reviewing your CPA reports. As noted before, a campaign can still be a success even if it doesn't have an immediate five-time (500%) return on investment. Not all marketing campaigns can break even from the get-go — that's why it's important to also know what each client has been worth to you over the long run and for how long. To calculate your ALCV, simply divide your total sales by the total number of clients — not the total number of leads — to quantify how much a client is worth to you.

While the reports outlined in this chapter will be incredibly helpful for you to start with, additional reports can be useful for reviewing the performance of your sales funnel at each step or progression. You would simply need to configure each CRM report accordingly. A lead magnet to tripwire conversion would ideally be the next report you'd put into place. In fact, having conversion reports for each stage would best indicate where you might need to fix your ascension elements.

If you are a service provider, the final reporting tool you will want to have is some sort of survey. A digital version would be best, because you would be able to accumulate the data without having to do much manual work, but anything is better than nothing. When setting up your client survey, you'll want it to ask about the referral source, and you should provide as many specific options as possible. Don't just list "the internet" as a choice — be more specific. Was it Facebook? Twitter? Google? An email? Delving deep into the true source of your referrals can be make-or-break for your marketing budget, and it's important you take the time to get answers to the right questions from the beginning.

Once you have the customer survey in place, you will have all the basics needed to report, review, and iterate your marketing program. You may find you have to do some manual work getting the numbers into a complete report, but tools do exist that can help gather all of your reporting data in a single place and present it in easy-to-read reports. For example, a tool called Graphly works incredibly well with Infusionsoft. It can calculate both your CPA and ALCV in real time, and can send out regular reports or links to data for your review at any interval or time you specify.

As a business owner, you have a multitude of things that need your attention, especially if you're a solo-preneur or are your own operation. So, the key to a reporting program is to have something that allows you to quickly ascertain whether your marketing strategy is working well.

STEP 8

DEVELOP AN EDITORIAL CALENDAR

Once you have the basic concept of your road map, your next step is to develop an editorial calendar of timely themes and special offers. Not only will this calendar help fill in some of the missing pieces of your core campaign approach, but it will help you with the special, ad hoc or "mini" campaigns that will drive further ascension of clients.

Not every person who opts in to your initial offer will immediately purchase. However, it is important for you to continue to market to these people through "remarketing" campaigns so that you can stay top-of-mind with the potential client until they are likely to purchase. An editorial calendar will help you focus efforts on these contacts as well.

For example, say someone opts in and gets your lead magnet e-book. If the person becomes a lead and is sent through the first tripwire sequence without purchasing, you want to make sure you have something in place to continually market to that person. You've likely paid money for them to join your list of warm traffic, and you want to continue your efforts to convert them into a paying customer. An editorial calendar is valuable in this regard because it gives you a pre-made angle or hook through which you can speak to the client again.

Typically, I recommend clients develop between a 12- to 24-month calendar. This calendar needs to set a theme for communication each month along with a call to action. Note that you are not looking to have a *sales* call to action each month — you don't want those on your email list to feel as though all you do is try to get money out of them. The majority of these calls to action should send them to free material that will increase their affinity for you and your business, all the while continuing to indoctrinate them toward working with you.

Your editorial calendar doesn't have to be set to just monthly sections. You can have weekly or quarterly entries depending on your sales cycle. A dentist should not push different specials each week given that the average customer comes in every six months. Conversely, a food service operation would be in terrible shape if its specials only changed every six months. You need to develop the calendar with some feel for how often your customers might be buying from you or how often they will want to hear from you.

Unsure how often people want to hear from you? Make sure you ask them on any opt-in form or new client documents you have them fill out, and then notate accordingly in your CRM system. The editorial calendar should not be used as a one-size-fits-all approach. In fact, for some clients I have worked with, we have developed multiple editorial calendars based on the different levels of customer engagement, services utilized, or frequency of service delivery.

The following steps will walk you through establishing your first-ever editorial calendar.

Step 1: Develop a list of services or keywords people will be searching for online when researching someone to buy from. The list can be any number of services or keywords, but making the list evenly divisible by the number of months you are planning ahead for can be helpful.

For example, if you are planning to create a 12-month editorial calendar, your list should ideally consist of three, four, six, or 12 items. It's not necessary, but having an evenly divisible number of topics will make for easier management. The key is to have at least one topic for each month or each time period.

Step 2: Create a document that lists out each service or keyword in a single column (an Excel doc or Google sheet is great for this). At the top of the column, put the header "Topics."

Step 3: Open a web browser and head to trends.google.com. This service is called Google Trends, and it will show you when people have searched for any keywords over the past 14-plus years (as of this writing).

Use this tool to see whether there is any seasonality to the searches people are doing for your topics and keywords. Determining whether there are times of the year when people are more likely to be looking for your services will be immensely helpful in planning the topics in your editorial calendar.

You will want to do a search for each topic you pinpointed. Set the time parameters to "all time," and then search for each of your keywords one by one. Put your findings into your Excel doc or Google sheet.

Step 4: If you find that any of your keywords/services have seasonal surges in search volume, make note of this in your document. For example, if the number of searches for one of your services spikes in June and December, include this information in your document. If there is no seasonality to a topic or service, note that as well.

Step 5: After you have researched every topic, using your data, select one topic for each time period. Schedule the topics with the highest seasonal searches first in your calendar. Make your way from most seasonal to least, and finish by making sure each time period has at least one topic.

Step 6: Come up with a call to action for each time period. Again, this doesn't have to be a sales pitch or offer every time. Free content or info works well toward building brand goodwill. You just need to make sure that each month, you present something for those you're communicating with to do that is in line with the topic you are promoting.

For example, each month should require an action on your clients' part. Whether a click, an opt-in, a call, or something else, you want to gauge level of interest by having participants take an action.

Step 7: Create a message (a blog, video, podcast, etc.) for each call to action. You don't have to fully develop each blog post or other message right now — just have an idea of what you are going to do and how you are going to promote it. For example, you might decide that you only want to have a blog and that each month you will promote it via email and your social platforms. That's fine — you just need to plan the promotion channels for each of your types of messaging.

Step 8: Designate who is responsible for putting the message together and pushing it out. You need to have accountability for this, and a great community or content manager can be extremely helpful in reaching your goals. If you don't have that person on your team yet, no worries — just make sure someone knows they're responsible for making the assembly and the sending of the message happen.

Once you have your editorial calendar in place, you will have completely finished all the planning for your marketing campaign. The rest of your efforts will be spent on real-world testing and traffic generation.

STEP 9

PLAN FOR TRAFFIC

By now, you have done all the work necessary to create a sustainable and successful marketing program. All that is left is to start sending traffic to your lead magnet, watching the data as it comes in, and from there developing iterations of your campaign's tactics. To me, this is the most exciting part of any campaign. After all the hard work you have put in, you finally get to see some financial results!

At this point, though, you are not quite ready to present your lead magnet to cold traffic. There are three types of media sources, and you need to test them in a certain order for maximum results while you're still working out any last-minute bugs or issues. The three types of media (or traffic) are owned, paid, and earned. Owned media refers to communicating with your audience via channels that you "own" — your email list, social media platforms, newsletters, etc. This traffic source should be the first one you use when you start turning on your marketing campaign — or, as I like to call it, your "money machine."

(A quick note: Traffic generation in and of itself is a huge topic and one that we are not covering in this book in a how-to sense. For this book, my intention is to explain how to manage it in setting up your marketing campaigns. Look for a book on generating traffic in the future.)

You need to be mindful of sending the right traffic to your lead magnet. If this lead magnet offer is one you have shown to owned audiences before, you will need to determine whether you want to show it again to your hot or warm audiences. If you send traffic or clients to something they have already seen, your results might be skewed negatively. On the other hand, if this is a completely new lead magnet, you will want to determine whether sending your entire list to it is truly appropriate.

Owned traffic is a great source of "test traffic" to run your marketing campaigns through first, as these people will be more forgiving of any hiccups they might encounter or missing details you might not have thought to include. A terrific way to frame the experience is that these people are getting special, first-time VIP access to your latest offer. The best practice is to send small segments of your list to the offer versus the entire list at once, so that you can run additional testing should your reporting show a cause for concern.

After you have run your owned traffic to your offer, you will want to review your reporting to see whether the numbers make sense and whether the campaign is performing as well as it should be. Keep in mind that when you use owned traffic, the majority of these people are part of your warm audience and will thus overperform when compared with cold traffic or audiences. So, if your ALCV is lower than your CPA (not ideal) when your offer is shown to a warm audience, you can almost guarantee this ratio will be worse when the campaign is shown to cold or paid traffic.

If your numbers end up not being where you want them to be, review your offer and start creating variations to test. Is the marketing message unclear? Is the value understated? Is your call to action button not working correctly? Identifying variations to test will help direct your next attempts on your quest to make your CPA and ALCV sustainable. Marketing optimization is yet another subject that could be a novel in itself and one that we won't fully address here.

Once your CPA and ALCV numbers are sustainable — you are getting more money out than what you are putting in — you will want to start testing paid media (traffic) to your offer. There are literally thousands of advertising options, and more so in the world of print media. My suggestion is that you start with Facebook ads. Simply put, there are millions of people on the website daily, the targeting options are incredible, and the cost to reach your ideal audience is affordable. You can start running ads for as little as $5 per day, and if you already have an existing client email list, Facebook can go out and find people who are just like your clients and show your ad to them.

Just like using owned traffic before, you will want to

send bursts of test cold traffic to the lead magnet and then review the data. If your numbers are still sustainable, you can then increase your ad budget until you start to see diminishing returns. You will probably find a limited number of targets on a social platform at some point, and you will then need to bring other outside sources into your marketing ad budget mix.

If your numbers are not sustainable, you will want to test variations of the ad, page, and offer like we did before with your email traffic, and work until the ALCV is greater than the CPA.

While I've mentioned that there are plenty of more in-depth resources when it comes to developing your Facebook ad campaigns, I have two pieces of advice to help you get started quickly. The first has to do with the basic structure of your ads and any sales copy you write, and the second is the different approaches your text ads can take to try to capture the attention of your cold traffic.

When it comes to sales copy, businesses have tried many different approaches. While that might sound like a total understatement, you should know that while there are innumerable ways you can approach your sales copy, one basic approach should be enough to get you started. In this three-step approach, the marketing message for your product or service needs to include (1) what it is you have, (2) how it can help the prospective customer, and (3) what you want them to do next in order to get it. This is a simple method that allows you to not only sell your items effectively, but that also allows for your natural voice to shine through.

The first part of this process depends on accurately describing what it is you offer or do. Your sales copy will be more effective if it is as accurate as possible and avoids vague generalizations. By being straightforward about what you offer, you help people quickly determine whether they want to consider buying from or working with you. The more people have to try to determine or infer what you are offering, the less likely they are to buy from you.

The second piece of this basic sales copy approach is to describe what the buyer will get when they purchase your product. Your sales copy needs to expand beyond just explaining just what the buyer will literally get — you want to take this description a step further by letting them know how you will solve their pain point. This is the customer's priority, and speaking to this key point will help you in converting the person into a buyer. As mentioned earlier, you will also want to talk about your customer satisfaction guarantees, as these will help dispel any buyer hesitation with regard to a potential negative experience.

The last piece of the sales copy you want to address is the action you want your customer to take. This should be the shortest part of the sales copy, and it should also be easy to highlight and direct your traffic to. Whether it's a button, a link, or something else, this is literally the shortest piece of the puzzle. Simply tell your audience how to take advantage of the offer!

These three pieces are the structure you will want to use for any ad and even your sales pages on your website. However, this structure needs to employ some basic selling approaches in order to truly grab the attention of your cold traffic. Here are three sales "hooks" you can use when developing your ads and associated sales pages for your products and services. The following sales hooks are courtesy of sales copy guru and my personal mentor, Frank Kern. (If you want to learn more about the sales copy writing process, I recommend learning from him.)

1: The gain minus pain. This simple sales hook helps you quickly communicate to your audience the key benefit you can provide while in turn avoiding a common pain point. Examples:

- How to increase sales without buying more ads

- How to get more traffic without more advertising

- How to earn a degree without going to college

- How to lose 12 pounds without exercising

Each of these hooks showcases a way a person can gain a benefit without a pain usually associated with gaining that benefit. The great thing about this hook is the versatility of it — you can use this theme in any number of media or presentations.

2: The truth about X. If you have a myth to dispel for your cold traffic audiences, this hook would be a good one to test. It's effective because challenging people's assumptions or beliefs is an excellent way to grab their attention. This hook works best for a lead magnet that would tie in thematically with your eventual tripwire offer. It also works best when it is tied to a pain point your customer is looking to avoid. Examples:

- The truth about amateur wedding photographers (and how to spot them)

- Why most personal training plans don't work

- The biggest thing you need to consider when scheduling your next oil change

3: What to do about X. This hook is a bit similar to the "truth about X" hook, but it is different in that it allows your customer to see a potential path forward that they can take through working with you. This hook is better to use when you want to highlight your expertise, and it works particularly well if your end goal is to get your cold traffic to sign up for a complimentary one-on-one session. Examples:

- Your first steps toward getting a divorce

- How to handle that stubborn belly fat

- The 3 most common growth mistakes businesses make

Using these three sales hooks along with the three-step sales copy approach will give you a solid start in developing your sales copy. Hiring a seasoned copywriter has its advantages in growing your business, but sometimes your budget has other ideas. You can use these suggestions as a basis, with reasonable confidence that you'll see some positive results.

Once your CPA and ALCV are sustainable, you can then work toward getting earned media. Think of earned media as coverage people give you for something worthy. This can be a newspaper article, a television appearance, a guest blog post, or anything in which someone else highlights your product or service. This kind of media is the best to get but takes the longest to realize and get sales from. Having someone on your team who can source earned media opportunities will be very helpful and profitable.

At this point, you have a fully functioning and potentially sustainable marketing program, and your focus can shift toward your testing and improvement efforts. Ideally, that will be the marketing phase you will spend most of your time on, working to boost the overall effectiveness of your marketing campaign.

STEP 10

TAKE IT TO THE NEXT LEVEL

Would you like me to double, triple, or even quadruple your marketing budget performance — for free?

From the desk of Thomas Holland

Dear friend,

I'm looking for a "dream" client for whom I can bring in massive windfalls.

If you're that client, I will personally work with you one-on-one in your business to help you double, triple, or perhaps even quadruple your revenue over the next 12 months. **You will pay nothing out of pocket, ever.**

Here's why.

The first thing I'm going to do for you is personally help you create a strategic plan to bring in immediate money. There's no charge for this, and it only takes about 45 to 60 minutes for us to do together. (After doing this type of thing for almost 15 years straight, I've gotten pretty good at fast results.) I'll even do most of the heavy lifting for you, telling you exactly what to send, how to position your offer, and how to bring in back-end money as well.

At the end of this initial planning session, one of three things will happen:

- You love the plan and decide to implement it on your own. If this is the case, I'll wish you the best of luck and ask that you keep in touch to let me know how you're doing.

- You love the plan and ask to become my client so I can personally help you execute, maximize, and profit from it ASAP. If that's the case, we'll knock it out of the park — and that's a promise.

- In the unlikely and unprecedented event that you feel like you wasted your time, I will send you $300 immediately, no questions asked. Your time is your most valuable asset, and I respect that.

It really is that simple, and there's no catch. Think about this: The worst that could happen is you get $300 for "wasting" 45 to 60 minutes of your time. The best that could happen is we work together one-on-one to increase your sales and profits several times over.

That's why this is the closest thing to *free money* you'll ever see.

Here's how it'll work:

First, we get on the phone and go over your business. I'll take a look at what you've got, what you're doing, and what you want to achieve going forward.

Once I have those "raw materials," I'll help you come up with a strategic plan of action to immediately and dramatically increase your profits.

There are a number of ways I might do this for you. For example, I might show you how to restructure your offer for a better price point, how to create recurring revenue (even without a continuity program), how to pull in buyers from untapped sources, or how to reactivate past customers.

And if you already have a list of prospects, we're bound to whip up a quick promotion you can run within days and that will have the cash register ringing over and over again.

And, like I said, there's no charge for this.

So why would I offer it?

Two reasons.

First of all, I enjoy it. This type of thing is what I do best, and it makes me very, very happy to see someone achieve financial success (and all that comes with it) as a result of the help I give them.

Second, it's how I attract consulting clients.

Here's how that works:

Assuming you're happy and you want me to crank out these types of plans for you all the time, you'll probably want to continue working together long term so I can help you implement them.

If this is the case, I might invite you to become a consulting client.

My "fee" is $3,000. If you think about it, though, it really won't "cost" you anything.

Why? **Because I expect to make you much more than $3,000 in the first six months.** And if we keep working together over the next 12 months, I'm confident I can perform even better.

Actually, I can give you a plan to make more than $3,000 during our first conversation, which is free! So, you'll see the value by the time you hang up the phone — without ever spending a dime.

And look, if you don't want to become a client, no worries. You won't get any sales pitch or pressure from me of any kind, ever.

In fact, here's my giant promise to you: **You will find our**

conversation to be incredibly valuable, or I'll pay you $300 immediately to compensate you for your time.

This is an amazing offer that you'll probably never see from any other "internet marketing consultant" in the world. Think about it: I'll personally generate a profit plan for you upfront — for free — and then let you pay me later if (and only if) you decide you'd like us to work together long term.

Plus, I'm taking it one bold step further by guaranteeing you'll find this free plan immensely valuable, or I'll pay you $300 for wasting your time. Just tell me, and it's yours. No questions asked.

Who else would do that? **NOBODY. (I checked.)**

But I'm happy to put it on the line like this because my consulting clients always stay with me, send in great feedback, and report terrific results. Period. Every single one of them. After all, I've worked with hundreds of businesses, and they keep looking to me for more.

My stuff works, and I know that if we work together, you'll be thrilled with the results we get for your business.

Consider this: Over the past five years, I've generated more than $3 million in sales for myself and my private clients.

As you can imagine, I'll get *a lot* of interest from this letter. And that's why I need you to read this next part carefully:

This is not for everybody.

I'm *very* picky about who I'll speak with, and I've got a strict (but reasonable) set of criteria that needs to be met in order for us to proceed. Here's who I can help:

- **You already have a solid business.** This offer is for people who are up and running and simply want to run a lot faster and a lot farther. Oh, and I won't work with beginners, get-rich-quick people, or "biz-opp" folks. No shenanigans.

- **You have a steady flow of leads and customers.** This means you're getting consistent traffic and are already making sales. You're running ads, you're promoting, and you're selling stuff. You don't have to be "everywhere" or "huge" — I just need you to be *present* in your market.

- **You have an email list.** It doesn't need to be that big — just responsive.

- **You have a good, solid product and a good reputation.** Everything we do together will not only be bringing you more sales and profits, but we'll be doing it in a way that creates massive goodwill in your market. And in order for us to do that, you need to have your act together. In other words, you need to be legit.

- **You follow directions.** (Don't worry; I won't ask you to do anything weird.) After all, if you don't actually implement the stuff I give you, neither of us will make money.

That's it! Those are all of my requirements.

If you meet the criteria I've laid out and would like to talk to me personally about getting you incredible results, I'll happily set aside some time for you.

Here's how the process works:

First, you'll need to fill out an application. I just need to know what you're selling, get an idea of what you want to accomplish, and get some other big-picture details.

I'm also going to ask for a "real person" deposit of $97.

Don't worry — I couldn't care less about your $97. I'm just using it as a "filter" to keep time vampires at bay.
I'll give it back right after we hang up (unless I take you on as a client, and in that case, I can apply it to your balance).

Once I have your application and your "real person" deposit, Jennifer from my office will call you to set up a time for us to talk. She's my "right hand" and my only employee, and she'll be contacting you within about 48 business hours.

Our initial call will be between 45 and 60 minutes. This is where we'll really begin working to figure out exactly what you want and how to make it happen.

I'll painstakingly review your goals, your offers, and so forth, and I'll deliver a plan to bring in money immediately.

If you see the value in becoming high-level client, great! We can talk about it.

And if at this point you don't want to become a client, that's OK too. I'll return your deposit as soon as we hang up. No biggie. And if you tell me I've wasted your time, I'll give you triple your deposit back immediately.

So, you literally can't lose. (By the way, I've never had anyone feel like their time was wasted — *ever*. That's why I can make this offer. I deliver. Would anyone else take such a risk?)

Warning: Time is a factor!

This opportunity is extremely limited because of the intense one-on-one time needed to provide you with results. Therefore, it is physically impossible for me to work with more than just a handful of people.

So, with that said, know that the window of opportunity is small.

If you think this is right for you, visit gthomasholland.com/apply, fill out an application, and let's talk.

Talk soon,

Thomas

P.S. You might be wondering what you "get" as a client. The main thing you get is me. Personally.

As I said earlier, our first conversation is free, and it will be about an hour or so. During this conversation, I'll give you a profit plan specific to your business based on what we talk about. I'll also give you some steps to take immediately for fast results. You get that first call regardless of whether you become a client.

Now, if you *do* become a client, we'll immediately schedule a follow-up call. On that follow-up call, we're going to come up with two things: a short-term cash flow goal, and a long-term income/lifestyle/business model goal. On the call, I'll give you specific action steps to complete to hit both goals.

From that point forward, two things will happen:

1: We'll speak every two weeks on the phone, monitoring your progress and tweaking where needed. This is one-on-one — not "group coaching" or anything like that. Just you and me focused on one thing: making you money.

2: We'll stay in constant communication via email. This way, I can see what you're doing and help you keep the momentum going between calls. I also use this as a way to review your sales funnel, opt-in pages, videos, etc. In fact, I often end up dictating sales copy and literally doing some of the heavy lifting for you this way. You can expect me to reply with voice memos, personal videos, and regular email responses.

The bottom line is: We're getting it done, constantly. Always building momentum and seeing constant improvement.

This is a genuinely rare opportunity. If you think this is right for you, visit http://gthomasholland.com/apply, fill out an application, and let's talk. Conversations are granted on a first-come, first-served basis.

ABOUT THE AUTHOR

G. Thomas Holland is the president of The Dark Horse Group LLC, a marketing consulting business that works with startups and small businesses.

When he is not writing, speaking, or working with clients, he can usually be found in the kitchen cooking or brewing. He is a journalism and history graduate of the University of Kansas, and Jayhawk basketball holds a special place in his heart behind only his family and the Chicago Cubs.

www.ingramcontent.com/pod-product-compliance
Lightning Source LLC
Chambersburg PA
CBHW060637210326
41520CB00010B/1640